Gatsby COCKTAILS

Gatsby COCKTAILS

CLASSIC COCKTAILS FROM THE JAZZ AGE

RYLAND PETERS & SMALL

LONDON • NEW YORK

Designer Luis Peral-Aranda
Editor Ellen Parnavelas
Head of Production Patricia Harrington
Art Director Leslie Harrington
Editorial Director Julia Charles

Indexer Hilary Bird

First published in 2012
by Ryland Peters & Small
20–21 Jockey's Fields
London WC1R 4BW
and
Ryland Peters & Small, Inc.
519 Broadway, 5th Floor
New York, NY10012

www.rylandpeters.com

The recipes in this book have been published
previously by Ryland Peters & Small.

10 9 8 7 6 5 4 3

ISBN: 978 1 84975 285 5

A CIP record for this book is available from the
British Library.

Library of Congress Cataloging-in-Publication
data has been applied for.

Printed in China

Notes
• When using slices of citrus fruit such as lemons or
oranges in a drink, try to find organic, unwaxed fruits
and wash well before using. If you can only find
treated fruit, scrub well in warm soapy water and
rinse before using.
• Measurements are occasionally given in barspoons,
which are equivalent to 5 ml or 1 teaspoon.

CONTENTS

THE GOLDEN AGE OF COCKTAILS

It was during the Prohibition era, which ran from 1920–1933, that cocktails really came into their own. Although the golden age of cocktails was probably between 1860 and 1920, it was arguably in the roaring 1920s that cocktails became very popular.

The Great Gatsby is F. Scott Fitzgerald's iconic novel, set in the 1920s at the height of the Prohibition era. It was a time of glamorous parties where bootleggers made millions selling their highly coveted illegally produced alcohol. *The Great Gatsby* is centred around one such bootlegger by the name of Jay Gatsby. In the novel, Gatsby is the mysterious host of many extravagant parties from the parlours of his luxurious mansion on Long Island, New York. There, he plays host to guests who have travelled far and wide to enjoy sipping cocktails and dancing under the stars until the sun comes up.

It seems rather unfortunate that this happy time in the development of the cocktail coincided with a most unhappy state of affairs in the USA. The Prohibition had a number of effects on drinking culture. It forced drinkers underground into illicit bars known as speakeasies, or decadent private parties such as those hosted by Jay Gatsby. These locations weren't dives, though – quite the opposite; they were luxurious and lavishly decorated and very female-friendly, which lent additional glamour to cocktails. Because liquor was illegal, inferior bootleg, or moonshine, was drunk, but was often so vile that bartenders would mix it with juices and cordials to mask its flavour. This was one of the reasons that cocktails became so popular. Many of the cocktails from this era were given seemingly innocuous names designed to fool the authorities, such as the Silk Stocking. Drinks would often be served in tea cups in an effort to disguise them from the police force.

Those bartenders who didn't wish to break the law during Prohibition hotfooted it to Cuba, or even further afield to Europe to ply their trade anew in a different country, but with as much enthusiasm as ever. This was a particularly creative time for them. Many of the drinks we count as classics today, from the Bloody Mary to the Sidecar, were invented overseas during that period, with the names of the bartenders who created them still hallowed in bars around the globe.

President Franklin D. Roosevelt had other ideas about Prohibition and it was repealed in 1933, shortly after he came to office. An accomplished drinker and handy bartender himself, FDR, along with Winston Churchill, was a great advocator of, among other cocktails, the martini. Indeed, it was during a summit meeting between Joseph Stalin, Churchill and Roosevelt in 1943 that Roosevelt first whipped up a round of Dirty Martinis for his companions.

Throughout the 20th century the cocktail has been through booms and slumps in popularity. It has adapted to social phenomena such as Prohibition, war, rises and falls of the stock market and the power of the media, and still flourishes in the 21st century, constantly evolving to suit our thirst for something new and different.

The glamour of the cocktail comes to life in this collection of authentic recipes from the 20s and 30s. Perfect the art of mixing period cocktails inspired by *The Great Gatsby*. Try serving up Jay Gatsby's tipple of choice the cooling Mint Julep, the classic Sazerac, or famous 1920s New York beverage, the Manhattan. Whether entertaining a few friends at home or hosting an extravagant Prohibition-style party of your very own, dust off your cocktail shaker and re-live the speakeasy experience with this collection of deliciously authentic cocktails.

JAZZ-AGE CLASSICS

'IN HIS BLUE GARDENS MEN AND GIRLS CAME AND
WENT LIKE MOTHS AMONG THE WHISPERINGS AND THE
CHAMPAGNE AND THE STARS.'

The Great Gatsby

SAZERAC

ONE OF THE EARLIEST RECORDED COCKTAILS, THE SAZERAC CAME INTO THIS WORLD SOME TIME IN THE 1850S. IT WAS ORIGINALLY MADE WITH BRANDY, BUT (AS I'M SURE YOU'LL AGREE) THERE'S NOTHING QUITE LIKE A GOOD RYE WHISKEY.

• • •

50 ml/2 oz. rye whiskey

10 ml/2 barspoons sugar syrup

2 dashes Peychaud's bitters

10 ml/2 barspoons absinthe, to rinse the glass

a thin lemon zest, to garnish

Serves 1

• • •

Stir all the ingredients, except the absinthe, in a mixing glass filled with ice. Rinse a chilled rocks glass with the absinthe. Strain the contents of the mixing glass into the rocks glass and garnish with a thin zest of lemon.

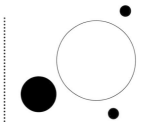

SIDECAR

THE SIDECAR, LIKE MANY OF THE CLASSIC
COCKTAILS CREATED IN THE 1920S, IS ATTRIBUTED
TO THE INVENTIVE GENIUS OF HARRY MCELHONE,
WHO FOUNDED HARRY'S NEW YORK BAR
LOCATED IN PARIS. IT IS SAID TO HAVE BEEN
CREATED IN HONOUR OF AN ECCENTRIC
MILITARY MAN WHO WOULD ROLL UP OUTSIDE
THE BAR IN THE SIDECAR OF HIS CHAUFFEUR-
DRIVEN MOTORCYCLE.

Shake all the ingredients together over ice and strain into
a chilled martini glass with a sugared edge.

• • •

50 ml/2 oz. brandy
20 ml/1 oz. fresh
lemon juice
20 ml/1 oz. Cointreau
sugar, for the glass

Serves 1

• • •

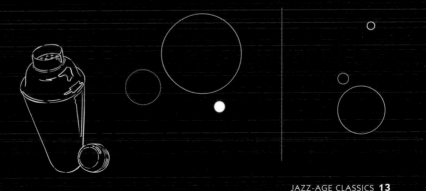

PERFECT MANHATTAN

THIS DELICIOUS COCKTAIL HAILS FROM THE BIG CITY JUST ACROSS THE WATER FROM JAY GATSBY'S LONG ISLAND HOME. 'PERFECT' DESCRIBES THE PERFECT BALANCE BETWEEN SWEET AND DRY.

50 ml/2 oz. rye whiskey

12.5 ml/2 barspoons sweet vermouth

12.5 ml/2 barspoons dry vermouth

2 dashes Angostura bitters

an orange zest, to garnish

Serves 1

Add the ingredients to a mixing glass filled with ice (first ensure all the ingredients are very cold) and stir the mixture until chilled. Strain into a chilled cocktail glass, add the garnish and serve.

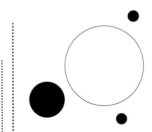

OLD FASHIONED

DURING THE PROHIBITION ERA, STRONG
FLAVOURINGS SUCH AS ANGOSTURA BITTERS
WERE USED IN COCKTAILS TO DISGUISE THE TASTE
OF ILLEGALLY-PRODUCED SPIRITS, OTHERWISE
KNOWN AS 'MOONSHINE'.

Muddle all the ingredients in a rocks glass, adding ice as
you go. Garnish with an orange zest and serve.

• • •

1 sugar cube
2 dashes Angostura
bitters
50 ml/2 oz. rye whiskey
or bourbon
an orange zest, to
garnish

Serves 1

• • •

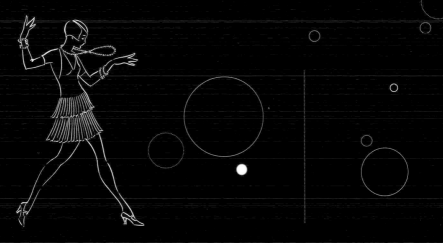

GIN GIMLET

A GREAT PARTY COCKTAIL TO SERVE ON A WARM SUMMER'S EVENING WHILE ENTERTAINING OUTDOORS – THIS DRINK NEEDS TO BE SHAKEN HARD TO ENSURE A SHARP FREEZING ZESTINESS.

50 ml/2 oz. gin
25 ml/1 oz. lime cordial

Serves 1

• • •

Add the gin and cordial to a shaker filled with ice. Shake very sharply and strain into a frosted martini glass.

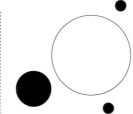

SILVER BRONX

THE BRONX DATES BACK TO THE DAYS OF PROHIBITION, WHEN GANG BOSSES REIGNED AND BOOZE PLAYED AN IMPORTANT PART IN THE ECONOMY OF THE UNDERWORLD. DIFFERENT AREAS OF NEW YORK BECAME KNOWN FOR THE SPECIAL COCKTAILS THEY OFFERED, SUCH AS THIS SPECIALITY OF THE BRONX.

Shake all the ingredients vigorously over ice and strain into a chilled cocktail glass.

• • •

50 ml/2 oz. gin

a dash of dry vermouth

a dash of sweet vermouth

50 ml/2 oz. fresh orange juice

1 egg white

Serves 1

• • •

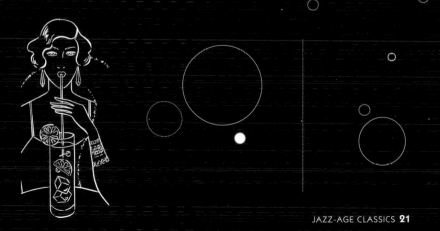

SILK STOCKING

35 ml/¾ oz. tequila

15 ml/½ oz. white crème de cacao

1 barspoon grenadine

15 ml/½ oz. double/ heavy cream

2 fresh raspberries, to garnish

Serves 1

• • •

THIS TEQUILA DRINK WAS INVENTED DURING THE 1920S, AT A TIME WHEN COCKTAILS WERE OFTEN GIVEN DECORATIVE NAMES REVELLING IN INNUENDO AND SENSUALITY.

Add all the ingredients to a blender. Add two scoops of crushed ice and blend for 20 seconds. Pour the mixture into a hurricane glass, garnish with two raspberries and serve with two straws.

JULEPS & SMASHES

'I BELIEVE THAT ON THE FIRST NIGHT I WENT TO
GATSBY'S HOUSE I WAS ONE OF THE FEW GUESTS
WHO HAD ACTUALLY BEEN INVITED. PEOPLE
WERE NOT INVITED – THEY WENT THERE.'

The Great Gatsby

MINT JULEP

THIS GRANDDADDY OF COCKTAILS WAS A FAVOURITE AMONG THE GUESTS AT JAY GATSBY'S INFAMOUS PARTIES. THESE DAYS IT'S A COCKTAIL FOR THE MORE DISCERNING AMONGST US.

• • •

15 ml/½ oz. sugar syrup
3 mint sprigs
60 ml/2 oz. bourbon

Serves 1

• • •

Muddle the sugar, one mint sprig and the bourbon in a rocks glass. Add crushed ice and garnish with the remaining mint sprigs. Serve with two straws.

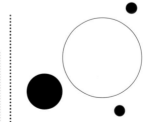

CHAMPAGNE JULEP

ADD A TOUCH OF SPARKLE TO YOUR EVENING
WITH THIS DELIGHTFUL ALTERNATIVE TO THE
TRADITIONAL MINT JULEP. IF YOU HAVE A BOTTLE
OF BUBBLY THAT HAS BEEN OPEN FOR A WHILE
AND LOST A BIT OF ITS FIZZ, DON'T WORRY; THE
SUGAR IN THE RECIPE WILL REVITALIZE IT.

Muddle the mint, sugar syrup and lime juice together in
a highball glass. Add crushed ice and the champagne
(gently) and stir well. Garnish with a mint sprig and serve.

• • •

5–10 sprigs of mint,
plus 1 to garnish

15 ml/1 tablespoon
sugar syrup

1 dash lime juice

champagne, to top up

Serves 1

• • •

MOJITO

THE MOJITO ORIGINATED IN CUBA AND IS THE
PERFECT DRINK FOR COOLING OFF AFTER A
NIGHT PERFECTING THE FAST AND FURIOUS
CHARLESTON ON THE DANCEFLOOR.

5 mint sprigs
50 ml/2 oz. golden rum
20 ml/1 oz. fresh lime juice
10 ml/scant 1 tablespoon
sugar syrup
soda water, to top up

Serves 1

• • •

Put the mint in a highball glass, add the rum, lime juice
and sugar syrup and pound with a barspoon until the
aroma of the mint is released. Add crushed ice and stir
vigorously until the mixture and the mint is spread evenly.
Top with soda water and stir again. Serve with straws.

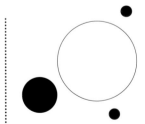

BOURBON COBBLER

FOR A DELICIOUSLY TROPICAL ALTERNATIVE TO
A MINT JULEP, TRY A REFRESHING BOURBON
COBBLER. GENTLY EASE THE JUICE OUT OF
THE FRUIT FOR A SHARP CITRUS FLAVOUR.

Gently muddle the fruit in a rocks glass, add the bourbon,
curaçao and ice and stir well. Add more ice and stir
again, garnish with a sprig of mint and serve with two
short straws.

...

a pineapple slice
an orange slice
a lemon slice
50 ml/2 oz. bourbon
15 ml/½ oz. orange
curaçao
a mint sprig, to garnish

Serves 1

...

(HAMPAGNE (OBBLER

a pineapple slice
an orange wheel
a lemon wheel
1 dash sugar syrup
champagne, to top up
a mint sprig, to garnish

Serves 1

• • •

TO CREATE A PERFECT PARTY COCKTAIL, ADD A TOUCH OF SPARKLE TO YOUR COBBLER BY REPLACING THE BOURBON WITH CHAMPAGNE. IF THE FRUIT IS NOT AS RIPE AS IT COULD BE, ADD A DASH MORE SUGAR SYRUP TO ENCOURAGE THE FLAVOUR.

Muddle the fruit together in a rocks glass. Add crushed ice and the sugar syrup and gently top with champagne. Stir gently and garnish with a mint sprig.

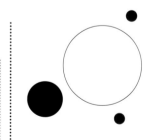

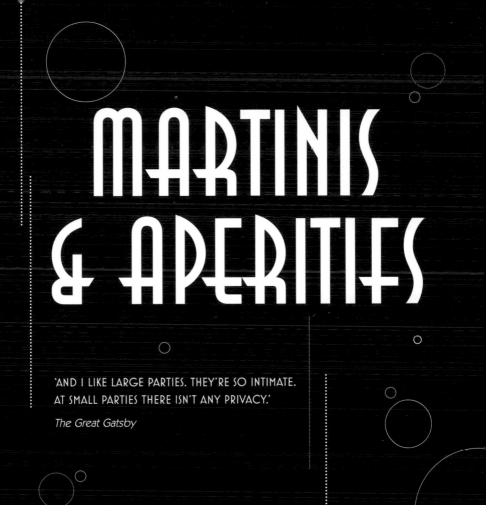

MARTINIS
& APERITIFS

'AND I LIKE LARGE PARTIES. THEY'RE SO INTIMATE.
AT SMALL PARTIES THERE ISN'T ANY PRIVACY.'

The Great Gatsby

ORIGINAL DAIQUIRI

THIS CLASSIC COCKTAIL WAS MADE FAMOUS AT THE EL FLORIDITA RESTAURANT, HAVANA, EARLY IN THE 20TH CENTURY. ONCE YOU HAVE FOUND THE PERFECT BALANCE OF GOLDEN RUM (TRADITIONALLY CUBAN), SHARP CITRUS JUICE AND SWEET SUGAR SYRUP, STICK TO THOSE MEASUREMENTS EXACTLY.

50 ml/2 oz. light rum
20 ml/1 oz. fresh lime juice
2 barspoons sugar syrup

Serves 1

• • •

Pour all the ingredients into an ice-filled shaker. Shake and strain into a chilled martini glass.

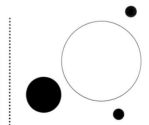

HEMINGWAY DAIQUIRI

LEGEND HAS IT THAT ERNEST HEMINGWAY WAS DIABETIC. SO THIS PARTICULAR DRINK WAS DEVISED FOR HIM USING MARASCHINO LIQUEUR AS A SWEETENER (THE SUGAR WAS RETURNED TO THE DRINK WHEN MADE FOR ANYONE OTHER THAN THE MAN HIMSELF!).

Add all the ingredients to a shaker filled with ice, shake sharply and strain into a chilled martini glass.

• • •

35 ml/¾ oz. white rum

15 ml/½ oz. maraschino liqueur

10 ml/2 barspoons grapefruit juice

10 ml/2 barspoons fresh lime juice

Serves 1

• • •

ORANGE DAIQUIRI

THE ORANGE DAIQUIRI SUBSTITUTES THE SWEET
MARTINIQUE RUM CALLED CREOLE SHRUB FOR
THE CUBAN RUM OF THE ORIGINAL DAIQUIRI
SO USES A LITTLE LESS SUGAR SYRUP TO KEEP
THAT DELICATE BALANCE OF SHARP AND SWEET.

• • •

50 ml/2 oz. Creole
Shrub rum

20 ml/1 oz. fresh
lime juice

1 barspoon sugar syrup

Serves 1

• • •

Pour all the ingredients into an ice-filled shaker. Shake and
strain into a chilled coupette glass.

CLASSIC MARTINI

THE CLASSIC MARTINI IS THE MOST ICONIC OF
ALL APERITIFS. STIRRING THE COCKTAIL TO MAKE
THE PERFECT MIX IS THE ORIGINAL LABOUR OF
LOVE FOR ANY BARTENDER.

Add both the ingredients to a mixing glass filled with ice
and stir. Strain into a chilled martini glass and garnish with
an olive or lemon twist.

• • •

a dash of vermouth
(Noilly Prat or Martini
Extra Dry)

75 ml/2½ oz
well-chilled gin
or vodka

an olive or lemon
twist, to garnish

Serves 1

• • •

DIRTY MARTINI

50 ml/2 oz. gin
1 dash dry vermouth
12.5 ml/2 barspoons
olive brine
a lemon zest, for the glass
a green olive, to garnish

Serves 1

• • •

THIS MARTINI IS ALSO KNOWN AS THE FDR AFTER
THE MAN WHO CALLED AN END TO PROHIBITION
IN THE 1930S. FITTINGLY, THE GREAT PRESIDENT
WAS AN ACCOMPLISHED BARTENDER WHO LOVED
NOTHING MORE THAN FLOURISHING HIS SHAKER
FOR ANY HEAD OF STATE WITH A LIKE MIND OR
A DRY PALATE.

Add the gin, dry vermouth and olive brine to a shaker
filled with cracked ice. Shake sharply and strain into a
chilled martini glass with a lemon-zested edge. Garnish
with an olive.

SMOKY MARTINI

THE MARTINI HAS SO MANY DELICIOUS VARIATIONS.
TRY USING A VERY SMOKY MALT, SUCH AS TALISKER,
OR A PEATED ONE, SUCH AS LAPHROAIG, FOR
INTERESTING RESULTS.

Add all the ingredients to a shaker filled with ice. Shake
sharply and strain into a chilled martini glass with a lemon-
zested rim.

• • •

50 ml/2 oz. gin
1 dash dry vermouth
1 dash whiskey
a lemon zest, to
garnish

Serves 1

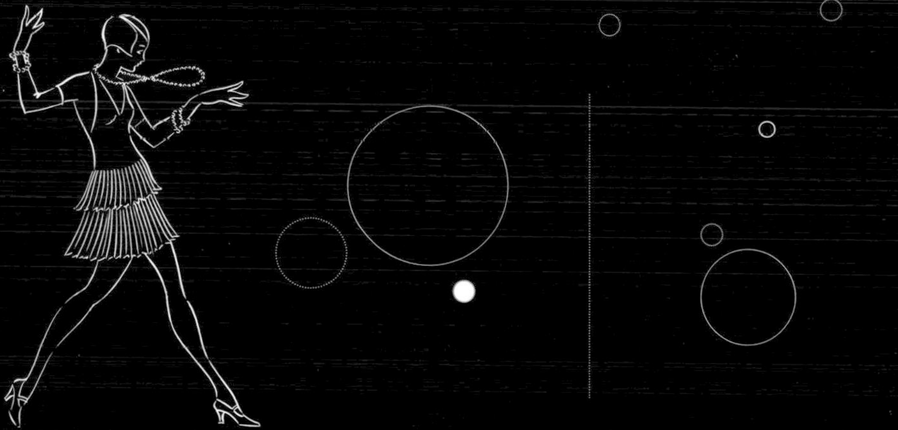

• • •

• • •

1 dash vermouth (Noilly Prat or Martini Extra Dry)

75 ml/2½ oz. well-chilled gin or vodka

silverskin onions, to garnish

Serves 1

• • •

GIBSON

THE LEADING THEORY BEHIND THE ORIGIN OF THIS CLASSIC MARTINI IS THAT IT WAS FIRST MADE AT THE BEGINNING OF THE 20TH CENTURY FOR CHARLES GIBSON, A FAMOUS ILLUSTRATOR, AT THE PLAYER'S CLUB IN NEW YORK.

Add both the ingredients to a mixing glass filled with ice and stir. Strain into a chilled martini glass and garnish with a few silverskin onions skewered on a cocktail stick.

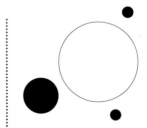

RICKEYS & FIZZES

'I WAS ENJOYING MYSELF NOW. I HAD TAKEN
TWO FINGER BOWLS OF CHAMPAGNE AND
THE SCENE HAD CHANGED BEFORE MY EYES
INTO SOMETHING SIGNIFICANT, ELEMENTAL
AND PROFOUND.'

The Great Gatsby

RASPBERRY RICKEY

THE RICKEY ORIGINATED IN WASHINGTON D.C. IN THE 1880S. IT WAS TRADITIONALLY MADE WITH GIN OR BOURBON WHISKEY, SODA WATER AND A LITTLE LIME JUICE. HERE, SOME RASPBERRY LIQUEUR AND FRESH RASPBERRIES HAVE BEEN ADDED TO ADD A SPLASH OF COLOUR AND A BEAUTIFUL BERRY FLAVOUR.

Muddle the raspberries in the bottom of a highball glass. Fill with ice, add the remaining ingredients and stir gently. Garnish with a lime wedge and serve with two straws.

• • •

4 fresh raspberries

50 ml/2 oz. vodka

20 ml/1 oz. fresh lime juice

1 dash Chambord

soda water, to top up

a lime wedge, to garnish

Serves 1

• • •

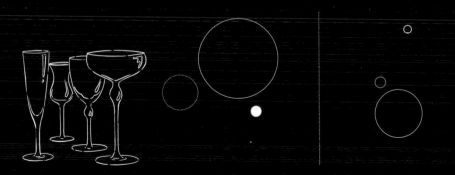

SLOE GIN FIZZ

50 ml/2 oz. sloe gin

20 ml/1 oz. fresh
lemon juice

1 dash sugar syrup

soda water, to top up

a lemon slice, to garnish

Serves 1

THE GIN FIZZ BECAME VERY POPULAR IN THE
UNITED STATES BETWEEN 1900 AND 1940. A
SPECIALTY OF NEW ORLEANS, WHERE DEMAND
FOR THE DRINK BECAME SO HIGH THAT
BARTENDERS COULD BE FOUND SHAKING THE
FIZZES UNTIL THE EARLY HOURS OF THE MORNING.

Add all the ingredients, except the soda, to a shaker filled
with ice. Shake sharply and strain into a highball glass
filled with ice. Top with soda water, garnish with a lemon
slice and serve with two straws.

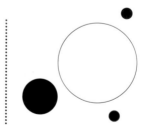

PEACH RICKEY

THIS FRESH PEACH RICKEY IS A GUARANTEED CROWD PLEASER. IT APPEALS DUE TO THE NATURE OF THE INGREDIENTS – THERE JUST SEEMS TO BE SOMETHING ABOUT PEACH PURÉE IN COCKTAILS THAT EVERYONE ENJOYS.

Build all the ingredients into a highball glass filled with ice. Stir gently and garnish with a thin peach slice or two.

• • •

50 ml/2 oz. vodka

20 ml/1 oz. fresh lime juice

15 ml/½ oz. peach purée

1 dash crème de pêche

soda water, to top up

thin peach slices, to serve

Serves 1

• • •

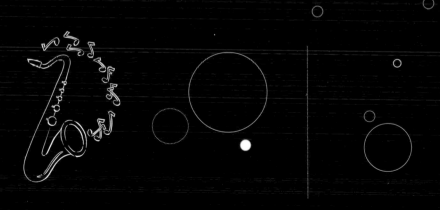

ROYAL GIN FIZZ

ADD A LITTLE CHAMPAGNE TO YOUR FIZZ AND YOU'VE GOT A ROYAL GIN FIZZ – THE PERFECTLY ELEGANT COCKTAIL TO HELP MAKE THAT OCCASION EXTRA SPECIAL.

• • •

50 ml/2 oz. gin

25 ml/1 oz. fresh lemon juice

1 barspoon white sugar (or 12.5 ml/½ oz. sugar syrup)

champagne

1 egg white

Serves 1

• • •

Put the egg white, gin, lemon juice and sugar into a shaker filled with ice and shake vigorously. Strain into a collins glass filled with ice. Top up with champagne.

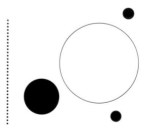

ELDERFLOWER COLLINS

THIS REFRESHING SUMMER DRINK IS A CLOSE
RELATION OF THE TOM COLLINS THAT
ORIGINATED IN NEW YORK IN THE 1880S. THE
BOTANICALS IN THE GIN GET AN UNEXPECTED
BOOST FROM THE ELDERFLOWER, MAKING THIS A
DELICATE COCKTAIL FULL OF FLORAL FLAVOURS.

Build all the ingredients into a highball glass filled with
ice. Stir gently and garnish with a lemon slice and a sprig
of mint.

...

50 ml/2 oz. gin

20 ml/1 oz. fresh
lemon juice

15 ml/½ oz.
elderflower cordial

soda water, to top up

sugar syrup, to taste

a lemon slice, to
garnish

a mint sprig, to garnish

Serves 1

• • •

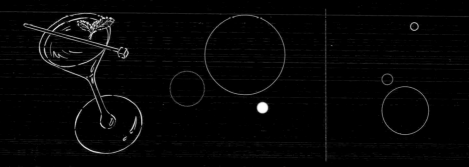

INDEX

CREDITS
All photography by
William Lingwood
All illustrations by
Rob Merrett apart from:
Pages 2, 36 and 52
Images courtesy of
The Advertising Archives
Page 8 Image courtesy
of Mary Evans Picture
Library
Page 24 At the Cocktail
Party, fashion plate from
'Art Gout Beaute'
magazine, March 1927
(pochoir print) by
French School, (20th
century)
Bibliotheque des Arts
Decoratifs, Paris, France/
Archives Charmet/ The
Bridgeman Art Library/
copyright unknown.
All best efforts have
been made to trace the
owner of this image.
Should you have further
information, please
contact us.